Dave Lambert

Fenimore Castle
A mystery for the stage

Ernst Klett Verlag
Stuttgart · Leipzig

1. Auflage   1 5 4 3 2 1 | 2016 15 14 13 12

Alle Drucke dieser Auflage sind unverändert und können im Unterricht nebeneinander verwendet werden. Die letzten Zahlen bezeichnen jeweils die Auflage und das Jahr des Druckes.
Das Werk und seine Teile sind urheberrechtlich geschützt. Jede Nutzung in anderen als den gesetzlich zugelassenen Fällen bedarf der vorherigen schriftlichen Einwilligung des Verlages. Hinweis zu §52a UrhG: Weder das Werk noch seine Teile dürfen ohne eine solche Einwilligung eingescannt und in ein Netzwerk eingestellt werden. Dies gilt auch für Intranets von Schulen und sonstigen Bildungseinrichtungen.
Fotomechanische Wiedergabe nur mit Genehmigung des Verlages.

© Ernst Klett Verlag GmbH, Stuttgart 2012. Alle Rechte vorbehalten.
www.klett.de

Redaktion: Virginia Maier

Satz und Gestaltung: Jacqueline Köhler
Illustrationen: Birgit Tanck, Hamburg
Druck: AZ Druck und Datentechnik GmbH, Kempten / Allgäu

Printed in Germany.
ISBN 978-3-12-560080-5

Contents

Before you read		4
Characters		5
Scene 1	In class	6
Scene 2	On the coach	8
Scene 3	A tour of the castle	9
Scene 4	Behind the Duke's painting	13
Scene 5	The Duke and Padlock	19
Scene 6	The castle dungeon	22
Scene 7	Back to our time	27
Activities		31
How to put on plays		37
Solutions		39

Before you read

1. *How is life today different from life in the 1500s? Make a list:*

   - We can ...
   - We can't ...
   - We've got ...
   - We don't

2. *The pupils in this story visit Fenimore Castle. Do you know a castle? Where is it? Tell your group about it.*

3. *Read the title and look at the picture on the front cover of this book. Also, read the text on the back cover.*

   a) *Look at the kids' faces. Do they look happy? How would you describe them?*

   b) *Look at the list of characters on page 5: Who do you think the kids are looking at?*

   c) *What do you think the story will be about?*

   d) *Look again at the title.*

   1. *What do you think the word "mystery" means?*

      1. Komödie ☐   2. Romanze ☐

      3. Geheimnis ☐

   2. Fenimore Castle *is a mystery for the stage. What do you think the word "stage" means?*

      1. Klassenzimmer ☐   2. Bühne ☐

      3. Kino ☐

Characters

Pupils in Class 7

Jamie ['dʒəɪmi]
Natalie ['nætəli]

Anna ['ænə]
Ricky ['rɪki]

Mr Watkins ['wɒtkinz], their teacher

At Fenimore Castle

The guide at Fenimore ['fenɪmɔː] Castle

The cook
Ben, a kitchen boy
The Duke of Fenimore
Padlock ['pædlɒk], his Chief of Police
Guards
Prisoners

---

guide [gaɪd] Fremdenführer(in) • **duke** [djuːk] Herzog • **chief of police** ['tʃiːf əv pəˌliːs] Polizeichef(in) • **guard** [gɑːd] Wachposten • **prisoner** ['prɪznə] Gefangene(r)

5

Scene 1 In class

Class 7 are getting ready for a visit to Fenimore Castle. Their teacher, Mr Watkins, is telling them about it.

MR WATKINS: Good morning, everyone!
CLASS: Good morning, Mr Watkins!
MR WATKINS: Now you all know that we're visiting Fenimore Castle tomorrow. What can you remember about it from our last lesson? Hands up, please!
ANNA: It's over 400 years old, sir.
MR WATKINS: Good, Anna.
JAMIE: It's the home of the cruel Duke of Fenimore, sir.
MR WATKINS: That's right, Jamie.
NATALIE: And it's 50 miles from our school.
MR WATKINS: Yes, it is, Natalie. Very good, everyone. Now, 400 years is a long time. How is our life today different compared to life in 1552? Hands up, please.
JAMIE: I think we have a better life now. Children today don't work like in the Duke's days.
ANNA: And we have better food to eat.
NATALIE: Yes, we can go to lots of shops where we can buy everything we want.
JAMIE: And we have a lot of modern things, sir.
MR WATKINS: Can you give me an example of a modern thing, Jamie?
JAMIE: Mobile phones. We can call people anywhere from everywhere!
MR WATKINS: *(Laughs)* That's right! Anything else?
JAMIE: We can watch TV. And we have cars, so we can go anywhere we want.

---

scene [si:n] Szene • **6 tomorrow** [tə'mɒrəʊ] morgen • **7 hands up** ['hændz ʌp] Hände hoch • **8 sir** [sɜ:] Anrede für den Lehrer • **10 cruel** ['kru:əl] grausam • **15 compared to** [kəm'peəd tə] im Vergleich zu • **21 modern** ['mɒdn] modern • **24 anywhere** ['eniweə] überall

Anna: Yes, but maybe we have too many cars now. There are so many in the town centre. And our towns are dirty.

Natalie: What about the Internet! We can write e-mails, find any information we need …

Anna: Maybe too much! The people then didn't have that problem!

Jamie: We can download cool music and listen to it everywhere.

Ricky: Yes, and we have games for our mobiles. I'm glad I live in our times and not in the boring old past! *(They all laugh.)*

Mr Watkins: Very good. So there are some good things about life in the past and some bad things. Now, when you are in the castle you can write down what you learn about the days of the cruel Duke for your project.

Natalie: I've got a digital voice recorder on my mobile, sir. I can record what the guide tells us about the castle.

Mr Watkins: Not a bad idea, Natalie.

Jamie: Can we use pictures for our project, sir?

Mr Watkins: Of course! Any other questions?

Ricky: Yes, sir, has Fenimore Castle got a dungeon?

Mr Watkins: No, it hasn't…

Ricky: But a good castle always has a dungeon!

Mr Watkins: Well, it has got one, but… that's the mystery.

Class: The mystery, sir?

Mr Watkins: Yes, we know there is a dungeon but nobody knows where it is.

Class: Really? / What?

Mr Watkins: That's right, nobody can find the dungeon. Let's look at a plan of the castle. *(He holds up a plan.)*

Anna: Look at all those tunnels!

---

9 **glad** [glæd] froh • 10 **past** [pɑːst] Vergangenheit • 16 **digital voice recorder** [ˌdɪdʒɪtl ˈvɔɪs rɪˌkɔːdə] digitales Diktiergerät • 17 **to record** [rɪˈkɔːd] aufnehmen • 20 **of course** [əv ˈkɔːs] natürlich • 21 **dungeon** [ˈdʌndʒn] Verlies, Kerker • 24 **mystery** [ˈmɪstri] Rätsel, Geheimnis • 26 **nobody** [ˈnəʊbədi] niemand

Natalie: And there are miles of corridors!

Mr Watkins: Miles and miles of corridors. So now you know why nobody can find the Duke's dungeon! That's the mystery of Fenimore Castle …

Scene 2 On the coach – the next day

Mr Watkins: Listen, class, when we get to Fenimore Castle, you all get off the coach and stay together so that you don't get lost. Ricky, are you listening or playing games on your mobile?

Ricky: I'm listening, sir. *(He's playing games on his mobile.)*

Mr Watkins: First, we have a tour of the castle. Now, it's very old and very, very big. As you know, there are many miles of corridors and tunnels, so we must all stay together. Ricky, put that phone back in your bag!

Ricky: Yes, sir. *(He puts it back in his bag.)*

Mr Watkins: Now, after the tour we go to the castle gardens to have our picnic lunch.

Natalie: Do we have free time after lunch, sir?

Mr Watkins: Yes, we do, Natalie. After lunch you have an hour to walk around the castle. You can visit the castle shop and buy a souvenir.

Class: Great! / I want to buy something really old. / I've got seven pounds fifty pocket money. / Maybe we can buy a book about the cruel Duke.

Mr Watkins: Now, remember, class, the coach leaves the castle at three o'clock. Don't be late!

Class: There it is! / Look, Fenimore Castle! / We're here!

Mr Watkins: Everyone off the coach now!

(The class gets off the coach and goes into the entrance hall of the old castle.)

---

1 **corridor** [ˈkɒrɪdɔː] Gang • **coach** [kəʊtʃ] Reisebus • 6 **to get off** [ˈɡet ˌɒf] aussteigen • 6 **to stay together** [ˌsteɪ təˈɡeðə] zusammen bleiben • 21 **something** [ˈsʌmθɪŋ] etwas • 22 **pocket money** [ˈpɒkɪt ˌmʌni] Taschengeld • 24 **to leave** [liːv] abfahren • 28 **entrance hall** [ˈentrəns ˌhɔːl] Eingangshalle

Anna: It's a massive castle. Look at the windows!
Natalie: And it's so old. Look at that door!
Jamie: It's easy to think you're really in the old days, the days of the cruel Duke.
Ricky: It's just a boring old castle and we can't even see a dungeon!
Jamie: Yes, but just think it's over 400 years old!
Ricky: Big deal! I like new things. Do you want to see the new game on my mobile? *(He takes his phone out of his bag.)* Look!
Jamie: How do you play it?
Ricky: It's a maze. It's almost impossible to find your way out! If you go into a dead end, you lose.
Anna: Oh, don't play games, Ricky. We're here to learn about the past.
Ricky: The past is boring!

Scene 3   A tour of the castle

The castle guide comes in.

Mr Watkins: Now, class, this is our guide. She can tell us everything we want to know about Fenimore Castle and life in the days of the Duke of Fenimore.
Guide: Welcome to Fenimore Castle, guys. We start our tour here in the entrance hall. Behind you is the castle shop. After the tour you can buy a drink from the drinks machine over there. Please follow me and stay with the group. These corridors are a maze. It's very easy to get lost.
Ricky: Hey, a maze, just like my new game!

---

1 **massive** ['mæsɪv] massiv • 8 **Big deal!** [bɪg 'diːl] *(informal)* Na und? • 12 **maze** [meɪz] Labyrinth, Irrgarten • 12 **impossible** [ɪm'pɒsəbl] unmöglich • 13 **dead end** [ded ˌ'end] Sackgasse • 13 **to lose** [luːz] verlieren • 21 **welcome** ['welkəm] willkommen • 21 **guys** [gaɪz] *(informal)* Leute • 24 **to follow** ['fɒləʊ] folgen

(The class follows the guide. Jamie, Anna, Natalie and Ricky are last.)
GUIDE: *(Standing in front of a painting on the wall)* This is a painting of the Duke of Fenimore Castle.
CLASS: Ugh!
GUIDE: Yes, he's an ugly man, isn't he? A very cruel man, too.
NATALIE: What has he got in his hand?
GUIDE: Oh, that's a key.
NATALIE: A key to what?
GUIDE: Well, nobody is sure. Look at it. It's very big and you can see a strange design on it.

RICKY: A strange design?
GUIDE: Yes, but we don't know what it is. It's another mystery.

---

3 **painting** [ˈpeɪntɪŋ] Gemälde • 6 **ugly** [ˈʌgli]] häßlich • 8 **key** [kiː] Schlüssel • 11 **strange** [streɪndʒ]] eigenartig, seltsam • 11 **design** [dɪˈzaɪn] Muster

ANNA: *(Looking at another picture on the wall)* Who's this, please?
GUIDE: Ah, that's the Duke's Chief of Police. His name is Padlock.
CLASS: Ugh! He's ugly too! *(They all laugh.)* 5
GUIDE: Follow me and I'll show you the kitchen.
MR WATKINS: *(To Jamie, Ricky, Anna and Natalie)* Stay with the group, you four! Don't get lost in the maze.
JAMIE: OK, sir. We're just looking at the paintings of the Duke and the Chief of Police. *(The others follow the guide but* 10 *Ricky, Jamie, Anna and Natalie are still looking at the paintings.)*
RICKY: These two give me the creeps!
ANNA: I'm glad I'm living now and not then!
NATALIE: Me too! 15
RICKY: Yeah. You can keep the past! No mobile phones, no games to download … really boring!
JAMIE: *(Looking at the painting of the Duke)* Hey, Ricky, this design on the Duke's key is like the maze in your game. It's got lots of dead ends. 20
RICKY: *(Looks at the key for a minute)* You're right, Jamie, it *is* a maze! Cool! Maybe it's a map of the castle maze!
JAMIE: And maybe that's the key to the dungeon!
NATALIE: Look here, maybe this is the dungeon in the centre of the design. If we follow it, maybe we can find it! 25
JAMIE: I'm taking a picture of the key's design.
RICKY, NATALIE AND ANNA: Yeah, great idea, Jamie. *(Jamie takes a picture).*
JAMIE: *(Looking at the picture with the others)* Hmmm … we are here, near the castle entrance hall. If we go 30 down here and left and right … *(They walk a bit.)*
ANNA: Hey, wait! Where's our class and the guide?…*(She calls.)* Guys? M-Mr Watkins?

---

13 **to give s.o. the creeps** [kriːps] jdm. Angst machen • 16 **yeah** [jeə] *(informal)* ja • 16 **You can keep the past!** [jə kn ˈkiːp ðə ˌpɑːst] Die Vergangenheit kannst du vergessen! • 31 **a bit** [ə ˈbɪt] ein bisschen

Jamie: Come on, we should go this way to find the dungeon!
Natalie: No … it's through here.
Ricky: It's this way, silly.
Anna: But where's our class? They can't all disappear!
(Everyone looks shocked.)
Natalie: This is weird. I don't like it.
Anna: We're lost in the maze!
Natalie: Well, you like mazes, Ricky. Get us out of this one!
Ricky: OK, OK … Let's go back to the painting of the Duke and start from there again. *(They go back to the painting.)* Now, let's follow the maze in the photo on Jamie's mobile again and see where it goes.
Jamie: Left… now right… No, that's a dead end … right again down this tunnel, right … right, … *(They come back to the Duke's painting.)*
All of them: This is seriously weird. / We're back at the painting of the Duke!
Jamie: But look at the photo of the maze. We should go straight on.
Anna: But we can't! There's a wall there with that painting of the Duke.
Ricky: I don't understand it, the map says go straight on.
Natalie: Maybe there's a door behind the painting!
Jamie: Good idea, Natalie, let's move it.
Anna: Don't be silly! If someone sees us …
Ricky: Anna, do you want to solve the mystery of the castle or not? Come on, let's move it! *(Ricky and Jamie move the painting.)*
Natalie: Look, there is a door behind the painting! Let's go through it. Come on! *(They go through the door and follow the map of the maze through many corridors.)*

---

2 **through** [θruː] durch • 4 **disappear** [ˌdɪsəˈpɪə] verschwinden • 6 **weird** [wɪəd] komisch, seltsam • 16 **seriously** [ˈsɪərɪəsli] *hier:* very • 22 **to understand** [ˌʌndəˈstænd] verstehen • 25 **someone** [ˈsʌmwʌn] jemand • 26 **to solve** [sɒlv] lösen • 27 **to move** [muːv] zur Seite bewegen

Scene 4 Behind the Duke's painting

JAMIE: Oh no, we're back at the entrance hall again!
ANNA: But look, the castle shop's not here now. And the drinks machine, where is it?
RICKY: There's just that old torch on the wall. And where are all the visitors? *(The cook comes down the hall.)*
ANNA: Shhh! Here comes someone now … Look, she's wearing old clothes … like in those paintings.
JAMIE: Hmmm … something is strange here. Let's follow her and see where she's going. *(They follow the cook through the entrance hall and down a corridor. She opens a big door and goes in. The children look in at the door.)*

---

4 **torch** [tɔːtʃ] *hier:* Fackel • 6 **Shhh!** [ʃ] Pst!

Cook: Where is that boy? He must wash the floor. It's dirty and the Duke wants his lunch. Boy, boy, where are you?
Ben: *(Coming out from under a big table)* I'm here, Cook.
Cook: What are you doing under there, boy? Wash this floor! Look at it!
Ben: I'm sorry, Cook. I'm so tired and hungry …
Cook: We're all tired and hungry in this castle. You can sleep tonight.
Ben: But my room is so cold, I can't sleep.
Cook: Get me some wood, boy. I need to cook! There will be trouble if the Duke's lunch is late. *(The boy goes out to get wood. The children hide in the corridor.)*
Ricky: Is this a joke? That boy … and the cook … they're talking about the Duke!
Natalie: And they're wearing clothes that make them look like the people in our books at school!
Anna: Maybe it's a show for the castle visitors? Yes, they all put on those clothes to show us life in the past. That's really cool!
Jamie: Hmmm … I hope you're right, Anna, because there's something strange here, something very strange … wait! Oh no! I think I know what it is!
Anna, Natalie and Ricky: What is it, Jamie?
Jamie: Well, first we follow the map of the maze on my mobile …
Anna, Natalie and Ricky: Yeah, what about it?
Jamie: … then our whole class disappears.
Anna, Natalie and Ricky: Yeah.
Jamie: Then we find that door behind the Duke's painting.
Anna, Natalie and Ricky: Yeah, and … ?
Jamie: Then, the shop in the entrance hall disappears.
Anna, Natalie and Ricky: Yeah, and … ?
Jamie: And the drinks machine … now there's just an old torch there.

---

1 **floor** [flɔː] Boden • 6 **hungry** [ˈhʌŋgri] hungrig • 8 **tonight** [təˈnaɪt] heute Abend • 12 **to hide** [haɪd] sich verstecken • 15 **to wear** [weə] tragen • 20 **to hope** [həʊp] hoffen • 26 **What about it?** [ˌwɒt əˈbaʊt ɪt] Was ist damit?

Anna, Natalie and Ricky: Yeah, and … ?
Jamie: Then we see that cook and the kitchen boy with clothes from the old days.
Anna, Natalie and Ricky: Yeah, AND … ?
Anna, Natalie and Ricky: JAMIE, WHAT ABOUT IT?!
Jamie: Well, don't you see?
Anna, Natalie and Ricky: NO, WE DON'T!
Jamie: We are all … back in the past!
Natalie: Back in the past? Don't be silly, Jamie!
Ricky: Are you telling me that the cook and the boy are really … people from the past?
Anna: Maybe Jamie's right. Look up there! *(They all look up.)* What can you see?
Ricky: Not very much, Anna. Duh! It's dark.
Anna: That's because there's no electricity, only some old torches and candles …
Natalie: Like in the old days … Maybe we *are* in the past.
Jamie: But when in the past?
Anna: And how?
Ricky: And how do we get back to our time?
Jamie: Look, the kitchen boy is coming back! Maybe he can help us. *(Ben is carrying lots of wood. The children come out.)* Excuse us … er … hello.
(Ben looks at the children in surprise. The wood falls to the floor.)
Ben: Oh! W-what do you want?
Anna: We … er … just want to talk to you.
Ben: Who … who are you all?
Anna: My name is Anna.
Natalie: And I'm Natalie.
Ricky: Hi, I'm Ricky.
Jamie: And my name's Jamie – er … what's your name?
Ben: … Ben.

---

12 **to look up** [ˈlʊkˌʌp] nach oben schauen • 14 **Duh!** [dʌ] *(slang)* Na klar! • 15 **electricity** [ˌelɪkˈtrɪsəti] Elektrizität • 16 **candle** [ˈkændl] Kerze • 17 **in the old days** [ɪn ði ˈəʊlˌdeɪz] früher • 20 **to get back** [ɡet ˈbæk] zurückkommen • 22 **to carry** [ˈkæri] tragen • 24 **in surprise** [ɪn səˈpraɪz] überrascht

15

JAMIE: Ben, can you help us? You see, we need to know something … something important.
BEN: What is it?
JAMIE: The date.
BEN: The date?
JAMIE: Yes, what's the date?
BEN: Well, it's the 14th I think.
JAMIE: The 14th of what?
BEN: June, of course. Don't you know what month it is?
ANNA: We're sorry, Ben, um … the 14th of June of what year?
BEN: I haven't got time to play silly games! I must hurry up and take this wood to the cook. The Duke wants his lunch!
ANNA: We'll help you. *(The children help Ben collect the wood.)*
NATALIE: Please, Ben, you don't understand … you see … we're from the future. We're visiting the castle with our class … and we're lost in the past.
RICKY: We need to know what year we're in.
BEN: Everyone knows it's the year 1552 …
ALL: 1552?!
JAMIE: But… but… that's over 400 years ago!
BEN: I don't understand.
NATALIE: Nobody does, Ben. One minute we're following the guide …
BEN: The guide …?
RICKY: Yeah, and the next minute we're back in 1552 with a lot of people in funny clothes!
BEN: *You've* got the funny clothes! Look at you all!
ANNA: I have an idea. Maybe if we go to the Duke he can help us.

---

17 **future** [ˈfjuːtʃə] Zukunft • 18 **to be lost in the past** [ˌlɒst ɪn ðə ˈpɑːst] in der Vergangenheit gefangen sein • 22 **400 years ago** [ˈjɪəz əˌɡəʊ] vor 400 Jahren

Ben: The Duke? Help you? *(whispering)* The Duke never helps people! If he finds you here, he'll throw you in the dungeon!

Ricky: So, there *is* a dungeon! That's so cool! We're solving the mystery of Fenimore Castle!

Ben: Of course there's a dungeon! That's no mystery. It's full of prisoners, but there are so many tunnels and corridors in this castle that nobody can find the dungeon to let the prisoners out. Only the Duke and his Chief of Police know where it is. And only the Duke has the key.

Natalie: That must be the big key in the painting!

Anna: You're right, Natalie. So it *is* the key to the dungeon.

Jamie: When we get back, we can tell everyone the answer to the mystery!

Anna: *If* we get back, Jamie. How do we get out of here? *(She looks at her watch.)* It's twelve o'clock now.

Ricky: That's why I'm so hungry! Let's have our picnic lunch.

Jamie: Ben, we can share our sandwiches with you.

Ben: Food! Oh thank you, my friends! I'm so hungry. I work in the kitchen, but I can never eat the food. I have to hurry! Cook is waiting!

Natalie: That Duke is a terrible man. *(They all sit down.)*.

Jamie: Here, Ben, have a sandwich.

Ben: A what? *(He takes the sandwich.)* It's bread … But it's so white! (*He starts to eat the sandwich.)* Mmmmm! This bread is so good!

Jamie: *(Thinks Ben is joking.)* OK, OK, I know, my mum's cheese and tomato sandwiches are boring…

Ben: Cheese and what…? *(Looks at his sandwich)* What is this red fruit?

---

1 **to whisper** [ˈwɪspə] flüstern • 2 **to throw in the dungeon** [ˌθrəʊ ɪn ðə ˈdʌndʒn] in den Kerker stecken • 7 **full of prisoners** [ˌfʊl əv ˈprɪznəz] voll Gefangener • 16 **to get out of** [getˌˈaʊtˌəv] *here:* entkommen • 17 **watch** [wɒtʃ] Armbanduhr • 20 **to share** [ʃeə] teilen • 26 **bread** [bred] Brot • 27 **white** [waɪt] weiß • 30 **tomato** [təˈmɑːtəʊ] Tomate • 32 **fruit** [fruːt] Frucht

Jamie: Tomato? Don't tell me you don't know what a tomato is, Ben!

Ben: Huh?

Ricky: You know, tomato, like in tomato sauce on pizza, mmm. It's not rocket science! Hey, if you guys don't have tomatoes, you don't have ketchup! Man!

Ben: *(Looking at Natalie's watch)* Natalie, can I look at that ... thing?

Natalie: What thing?

Ben: The little machine…on your arm …

Natalie: Oh … Yes, of course.

Ben: What is it?

Natalie: It's a watch. It tells you the time.

Ben: And who is this on it?

Natalie: Oh, that's Mickey Mouse.

Ben: Mickey who?

(They all laugh.)

Anna: In our time, Ben, there are many modern things, things you don't have now.

Ben: Really?

Natalie: Yeah, like digital voice recorders. *(She takes out her mobile.)* Listen!

Anna's voice: Who's this, please?

Guide's voice: Ah, that's the Duke's Chief of Police. His name is Padlock.

Children's voice: Ugh, he's ugly too! *(We hear the children laugh.)*

Ben: *(looks around)* W-who said that!

Natalie: It's only my mobile, look.

Ben: Stop that thing! If the Chief of Police hears it, he'll throw us all in the dungeon! I don't understand. The future is a very strange place.

Ricky: Well, it's better than the past, Ben. We've got ketchup. Hey, look at this. *(Ricky shows Ben the game on his*

---

5 **It's not rocket science!** [ɪts ˌnɒːt ˈrɒkɪt ˌsaɪəns] (informal) Das ist doch nun wirklich nicht so kompliziert! • 13 **It tells you the time.** [ɪt ˌtelz jə ðə ˈtaɪm] Sie zeigt dir die Uhrzeit an. • 23 **voice** [vɔɪs] Stimme

mobile.) Try to get out of the maze. *(Ben starts to play the game. They hear the cook's voice.)*

COOK: Boy! Where are you, boy? Bring me that wood now!
BEN: Oh no, it's Cook! Wait here for me. Maybe I can help you. *(To the cook)* I'm coming! *(He runs to the kitchen with the wood.)*
NATALIE: Poor Ben. Kids in 1552 have a really hard life.
RICKY: It's not all bad, Natalie. Ben hasn't got boring old school. And no boring old history teachers like Mr Watson.
ANNA: Listen! Someone's coming. Let's hide! *(The children run into the dining room and hide.)*

Scene 5   The Duke and Padlock

The Duke enters the dining room. With him is Padlock, the Chief of Police, and some guards. The Duke sits down. The others stand.

DUKE: Tell me, Padlock, how are things in my castle?
PADLOCK: Well, sire … I'm sorry, but food is disappearing.
DUKE: *(Angry)* Disappearing?
PADLOCK: Yes, sire. Someone is stealing it from the castle kitchen.
DUKE: Stealing my food!
PADLOCK: Yes, sire … In this last week, *(he reads from a list)* … 50 pounds of apples, 10 pounds of cheese, bread, butter, sausages … But worst of all, someone is stealing that new fruit we have … The present from the King of Spain!

---

9 **history** [ˈhɪstri] Geschichte • 12 **dining room** [ˈdaɪnɪŋ ˌruːm] Speisesaal • 16 **How are things …** [ˈhaʊ ə ˌθɪŋz] Wie läuft es … • 17 **sire** [ˈsaɪə] Durchlaucht • 18 **angry** [ˈæŋgri] zornig • 19 **to steal** [stiːl] stehlen • 23 **pound** [paʊnd] Pfund (454 g) • 24 **sausage** [ˈsɒsɪdʒ] Wurst • 24 **worst of all** [ˌwɜːst əv ˈɔːl] was am Schlimmsten war

Duke: My ... my ... tom-tom-...

Padlock: Your tomatoes, sire, to-ma-toes. Yes!

Duke: Padlock, you are my Chief of Police. You must find the thief right now and throw him or her in the dungeon!

Padlock: Yes, yes, sire, of course, sire ... er ... there is just one small problem with the dungeon, sire.

Duke: Problem with the dungeon!?

Padlock: Yes, sire, you see, there's no room for more prisoners. It's full.

Duke: Well, make more room, you idiot!

Padlock: Yes, sire, of course, sire, how silly of me, sire.

Duke: And Padlock?

Padlock: Y-yes, sire?

Duke: If you don't find the thief right now, I'll throw you in the dungeon, too!

Padlock: Oh yes, sire, of course, sire.

(The door opens. Ben comes in.)

Ben: Lunch is ready, sire.

Duke: Good. You can go, boy.

Padlock: *(Looking at Ben)* Just a moment, sire, I want to talk to this boy. You work in the kitchen, don't you, boy?

Ben: Y-yes, I do.

Padlock: Hmmm ... *(Looking at his list)* Tell me, do you like apples?

Ben: Oh yes, I do.

Padlock: Hmmm ... what about sausages?

Ben: I *love* sausages!

Padlock: And bread and cheese with lots and lots of butter?

Ben: Oh yes, yes, I love all those things!

Padlock: Thank you. *(To the Duke)* Do you need to hear more, sire?

Duke: I don't understand, Padlock. What are you doing?

Padlock: It's very simple, sire. Food is disappearing from the kitchen. This boy works in the kitchen. Look at the

---

8 **there's no room** [ðez nəʊ 'ruːm] es gibt keinen Platz (mehr) • 9 **full** [fʊl] voll • 10 **idiot** ['ɪdiət] Idiot • 14 **to throw s.o. in the dungeon** [ˌθrəʊ ɪn ðə 'dʌndʒn] jdn. in den Kerker werfen • 33 **simple** ['sɪmpl] einfach

list. He says he loves all the things on it … there is your thief, sire!

Duke: Very clever, Padlock, very clever.

Padlock: Oh, sire, thank you.

Duke: But, just a moment, Padlock…this boy can't be eating all that food. Look at him. He's too thin!

Padlock: True, sire, he is thin. But still …

Duke: And I don't care about sausages and cheese and apples! I want to know who is stealing my tom-tom- … my tom … you know, the new fruit! What do you call them?

Padlock: Tomatoes, sire?

Duke: Yes, that's it … Them.

Padlock: Come here, boy. *(Ben goes to Padlock. He is very scared.)* Open your mouth and say Ahh!

Ben: Ahh!

Padlock: *(sniffs)* Ye-ees! I can smell tomatoes! Here is your thief, sire!

6 **thin** [θɪn] dünn • 7 **true** [truː] *hier:* richtig • 7 **but still** [bət ˈstɪl] trotzdem • 8 **I don't care** [ˌaɪ dəʊntˈkeə] es ist mir egal • 15 **mouth** [maʊθ] Mund • 17 **to sniff** [snɪf] riechen

BEN: No, no, I can explain everything! Jamie's mother … she made bread and cheese with –
DUKE: Guards! Throw the boy in the dungeon! Ha ha ha!
BEN: I'm not a thief! Don't throw me in the dungeon! *(The guards take Ben.)*
DUKE: All this talk about food is making me hungry. Cook! Bring me my lunch! *(The Duke eats noisily. Padlock watches. The kids whisper.)*
JAMIE: Poor Ben, down in the dungeon! And all because of mum's boring old cheese and tomato sandwiches!
ANNA: What can we do?
RICKY: We must find the dungeon and let him out. We've got a picture of the maze.
JAMIE: But the Duke's got the key.
ANNA: How can we get it?
RICKY: Easy! We hide in the Duke's bedroom and when he's sleeping we take it from him.
ANNA: Oh yes, Ricky, very easy! If the Duke wakes up, he'll throw us in the dungeon, too!
JAMIE: Maybe he sleeps after lunch. Let's hide in his bedroom now!

(They tiptoe out the door.)

Scene 6   The castle dungeon

The Duke's bedroom. The Duke is in his pyjamas. He is getting ready for bed.

DUKE: A nice lunch. A very good morning. Another prisoner for my dungeon. Now, who else can I put in there? Padlock? Hmmm … no, I need him. I know: those silly guards. I think maybe it's time for them to go in the

---

7 **noisily** ['nɔɪzɪli] geräuschvoll • 8 **to whisper** ['wɪspə] flüstern • 22 **to tiptoe out** ['tɪptəʊ] hinausschleichen • 23 **pyjamas** [pɪ'dʒɑːməz] Schlafanzug • 26 **who else** [huˈels] wer sonst noch

dungeon. Ha ha ha! *(He gets into bed.)* I'm so cruel, I really don't know how I do it! … Ah, the key to the dungeon. Here it is. Nobody can find it if I put it here under my pillow.

(When the Duke is sleeping, the children come out from behind a cupboard.)

JAMIE: *(Whispering)* The Duke wants to put his guards in the dungeon!

NATALIE: Yeah, and I've got every word here *(Shows her mobile)*.

ANNA: Great, Natalie! Maybe we can use it later.

RICKY: Why is the Duke in his pyjamas?

JAMIE: Shhh … Duh, because he's sleeping.

RICKY: It's two o'clock in the afternoon. Weird!

ANNA: Shhh! The important thing is he's sleeping, Ricky! Now get the key. You heard him! It's under his pillow!

RICKY: OK, OK. *(Ricky and the others go on tiptoe to the bed and he puts his hand under the Duke's pillow.)*

JAMIE: Be careful, Ricky! Don't wake him up.

16 **pillow** ['pɪləʊ] Kissen • 17 **on tiptoe** ['tɪptəʊ] auf Zehenspitzen • 19 **Be careful!** [bɪ 'keəfl] Pass auf!

Natalie: Shhh…
(The Duke turns over.)
Natalie: Phew!
Jamie: Try again, Ricky.
Anna: Shhh … *(Ricky puts his hand under the pillow again.)*
Duke: Mummy!
Natalie: Is he asleep?
Anna: I … I think so. Try again, Ricky.
Ricky: *(Ricky gets the key.)* I've got it, I've got the key, and look, it's got the same design!
Anna: Just like the key in the painting!
Jamie: Well done!
Ricky: Let's get out of here! *(They run out of the Duke's bedroom.)*
Anna: We'll follow the design on the key to the centre of the castle. That must be the dungeon.
Jamie: Let's go this way!
(They run down many tunnels. They come to the dungeon. Some guards are standing at the door. The kids are hiding around the corner.)
Anna: *(Whispering)* Look, it's the dungeon! And it's full of prisoners! And there's Ben!
Jamie: But how can we let them out? Those guards are not nice.
Natalie: Or very intelligent …. Hey, I've got an idea. *(Natalie starts to go.)*
Jamie: Natalie, come back! What are you doing?
Natalie: *(Goes to the guards)* Hello, guards!
Guards: Huh? What are you doing here? Let's put her in the dungeon with the others!
Natalie: Wait a minute. You are the Duke's guards, aren't you?
Guards: Aye, we are.

---

2 **to turn over** [tɜːn ˈəʊvə] sich umdrehen • 3 **Phew** [fjuː] Puh! • 4 **Try again** [ˌtraɪ əˈɡen] versuch es nochmal • 12 **Well done!** [wel ˈdʌn] Gut gemacht! • 13 **Let's get out of here!** [lets ɡet ˌaʊt əv ˌhɪə] Lass uns abhauen! • 20 **corner** [ˈkɔːnə] Ecke • 25 **intelligent** [ɪnˈtelɪdʒnt] intelligent • 33 **Aye!** [aɪ] Jawohl!

NATALIE: Do you know that the Duke wants to put you guards in the dungeon?
GUARDS: What? The Duke is our friend ...
NATALIE: No, he isn't! He and Padlock are cruel men.
GUARDS: She's just saying that. Let's throw her in the dungeon!
NATALIE: Wait! Look what I have here! *(She shows them her mobile).*
GUARDS: Huh? What's that?
NATALIE: It's a mobile phone, and it's got a digital voice recorder.
GUARDS: Huh? W-what?
NATALIE: Listen, you can hear your "friend", the Duke.
THE DUKE'S VOICE: Now, who else can I put in my dungeon? Padlock? Hmmm ... no, I need him. I know: those silly guards. I think maybe it's time for them to go to the dungeon, too. Ha ha ha!
NATALIE: You see? The Duke is not your friend.
GUARDS: She's right! Come on, boys, let's get him!
(Jamie and the others come out.)
JAMIE: Wait, we've got the key to the dungeon. We can let all the prisoners out.
BEN: Look, everyone, these are my friends, the children from the future!
PRISONERS: Let us out, let us out, open the door!
(Jamie opens the door and the prisoners come out.)
PRISONERS: We're out, we're out, hooray!
BEN: Thank you!
ANNA: Now we have another little job to do. Come on, everyone, let's give the Duke and Padlock a surprise.
GUARDS: Follow us, we know the way!
PRISONERS: Come on, let's go! Let's find the Duke! Let's find Padlock! *(They all run out.)*

---

19 **to get s.o.** [ˈgɛt sʌmwʌn] *hier:* jdn. packen

The Duke's bedroom. The Duke is in bed sleeping. The children, some guards and some prisoners run in.

DUKE: *(Waking up and looking at them all)* HUH? Help! Help! It must be a dream! Guards, guards!
GUARDS: Here we are! So, you want to put us in the dungeon, do you?
DUKE: N-no, of course not! Padlock, where are you?
(Another group of prisoners and guards comes in with Padlock.)
PADLOCK: I'm here, sire! They have me too! And there are guards with them!
GUARDS: Let's put these two in the stocks!
EVERYONE: The stocks! The stocks!
DUKE AND PADLOCK: No, no, not the stocks! Please, not the stocks!
(They put the Duke and Padlock in the stocks.)

12 **stocks** [stɒks] Pranger

BEN: *(To the Duke and Padlock)* I am not a thief. All these prisoners are good people, but you are bad and cruel men.

COOK: Let's leave these two here. Come on everyone, you must be hungry. There's lots of delicious food in the castle kitchen.

EVERYONE: Food! *(They all run to the castle kitchen.)*

Scene 7 Back to our time

Everyone is sitting at the table in the castle kitchen. They're all eating and drinking.

BEN: All this food! Sausages, cheese, eggs and apples!
COOK: And tomatoes from the King of Spain!
RICKY: Now you can make ketchup, Cook. And pizza!
ANNA: *(To Ben)* Well, thanks for lunch, Ben. It's time for us to go back to our time now. Our coach leaves the castle at three o'clock.
JAMIE: We must find that door behind the Duke's painting. Take the key to the dungeon, Ben. *(He gives Ben the key.)*
BEN: Thank you! Now we can close the tunnel to the dungeon so that nobody can use that terrible place again.
RICKY, JAMIE, ANNA, NATALIE: That's a great idea, Ben.
RICKY: Here, Ben, this is for you, too. *(He gives Ben his mobile phone.)*
BEN: Oh, thank you, Ricky!
RICKY: That's OK. I never want to see another maze again!
(They all laugh.)

---

4 **to leave** [liːv] *hier:* lassen • 5 **delicious** [dɪˈlɪʃəs] köstlich, lecker • 20 **so that** [ˈsəʊ ðət] damit

RICKY, JAMIE, ANNA, NATALIE: Goodbye, Ben, goodbye, everyone!

EVERYONE: Goodbye, and thank you! *(Ricky, Anna, Natalie and Jamie leave and walk down a corridor.).*

RICKY: This way?

ANNA: No, it's a dead end, Ricky.

JAMIE: Follow me. The map of the maze says it's this way. *(They walk down many corridors.)*

NATALIE: Hey, look, the map's right! There's the door behind the painting of the Duke. Our time should be on the other side!

ANNA: Come on, let's go through it!

(They go through it.)

JAMIE: We're back in our time!

RICKY, JAMIE, ANNA, NATALIE: We're back, we're back!

RICKY: At the end of that corridor is the castle entrance hall! *(They run into the castle entrance hall.)*

RICKY: And there's the castle shop!

ANNA: And the drinks machine!

NATALIE: Oh, look, it's 3 o'clock. The coach is leaving for school. Come on!

(They run to the coach. The class is waiting there with Mr Watkins and the guide.)

MR WATKINS: Come on, you four! All the class is waiting for you.

RICKY, JAMIE, ANNA, NATALIE: Sir, sir, we know the answer to the mystery of Fenimore Castle!

GUIDE, CLASS, MR. WATKINS: You what? / Really? / What is it? / Tell us!

RICKY: There is a dungeon, a big one! It's in the centre, down under the castle!

GUIDE: But how do you kids know all this?

CHILDREN: The answer's in the key.

---

11 **other side** [ʌðə ˈsaɪd] andere Seite

Mr Watkins: What key?
Anna: The key in the painting of the Duke, of course.
Ricky: The design on the key is a map of the castle maze. It shows you the way through all the corridors and tunnels.
Natalie: And it takes you straight behind that painting of the Duke …
Guide: Behind the painting? But … but how?
Jamie: If you move the painting, there's a door behind it.
Everyone: A door?
Ricky: Yeah, and it takes you to the dungeon!
Guide: Oh, this is exciting! Let's go and see the dungeon now.
Jamie: Er … you can't.
Guide, Mr Watkins: Why not?
Jamie: Well, you see, it's closed. There's a wall over the tunnel now.
Guide: Of course, a tunnel, a wall!
Anna: Yes, it was Ben's idea. So nobody can use that terrible place again.
Ricky: That's why nobody can find the dungeon today.
Guide: Of course! You kids have the answer to the mystery of Fenimore Castle! Well done! I'm going to phone the newspaper and the TV stations! *(She runs to the castle.)*
Mr Watkins: But, but, who is Ben …? He's not in our class, is he?
Ricky: No, sir, he's the Duke's kitchen boy.
Mr Watkins: The Duke's kitchen boy … ?
Ricky: Yeah, he's from the past. He's very nice but he doesn't know what pizza or cheese and tomato sandwiches are. And he doesn't even know who Mickey Mouse is!

---

12 **exciting** [ɪkˈsaɪtɪŋ] aufregend • 16 **closed** [kləʊzd] zugemauert • 24 **newspaper** [ˈnjuːsˌpeɪpə] Zeitung • 24 **TV station** [tiːˌviː ˈsteɪʃn] Fernsehsender

Mr Watkins: Mickey Mouse … ? I'm too tired to understand this now, Ricky. Everyone on the coach! *(They all get on the coach. Mr Watkins speaks to Ricky before he gets in.)* Oh, and Ricky, absolutely no games on your mobile until after we get back to school, understand?
Ricky: Oh, I haven't got my mobile, sir.
Mr Watson: Ricky! It's in the castle, isn't it!
Ricky: Yes, Ben has got it, sir.
Mr Watkins: Ben?
Ricky: Yeah, you know, the boy from the past?
Mr Watkins: Ooh! Tell us all about it in class tomorrow, Ricky. On the coach!
Ricky: OK, sir. *(He talks as he gets in the coach.)*
Ricky: Uh … sir, do you know, after our visit to Fenimore Castle, I don't think the past is so boring after all!

2 **On the coach!** [kəʊtʃ] Einsteigen! • 4 **absolutely no games** [ˌæbsəˈluːtli nəʊ ɡeɪmz] du darfst überhaupt keine Spiele spielen

Activities

Scene 1

1. *"We have a lot of modern things" (Jamie, p. 6). Make a list of what the kids say. Now look at your list from "Before you read" and this one. Which things are the same? Which are different?*

2. *What is the mystery of Fenimore Castle?*

Scene 2

1. *Does Ricky find the castle interesting? Why or why not?*

2. *You have £7.50 pocket money. What do you want to buy in the castle shop? Say why.*

   - a Fenimore Castle T-shirt
   - a poster of the Duke
   - a book about the castle
   - a DVD about life in 1552

3. *What do these words mean in German? Choose a meaning for every word.*

coach	etwas
entrance hall	Irrgarten
maze	Reisebus
dead end	Eingangshalle
to leave	Sackgasse
something	abfahren

Scene 3

1. *Who are the people in the paintings?*

2. *What is special about the key?*

3. *Why does Jamie take a picture of the key? How do the kids use this picture?*

4. *Why do the kids move the painting of the Duke?*

Scene 4

1. *How do the kids know they are in the past?*

2. *Who is Ben, and what does he tell them about the dungeon?*

3. *Ben does not know many things from our time. What are they?*

Scene 5

Answer these questions:

   a) *What is happening in the Duke's kitchen?*

- [ ] 1. Someone is eating.
- [ ] 2. The food is bad.
- [ ] 3. Someone is stealing the food.

b) *Which special food does the Duke have in his kitchen?*

☐ 1. apples
☐ 2. tomatoes
☐ 3. ice cream
☐ 4. milk

c) *Why must Padlock find the thief?*

☐ 1. Then the Duke will give him money.
☐ 2. He wants to help the Duke.
☐ 3. If he doesn't find the thief, the Duke will throw Padlock in the dungeon.

d) *When Padlock smells tomatoes, what happens?*

☐ 1. Padlock asks Ben where he got them.
☐ 2. Padlock tells the Duke that Ben must be the thief.
☐ 3. Padlock tells Ben that his mouth smells bad.

Scene 6

Some of these sentences are correct and others have wrong information. Correct the wrong sentences.

a) The Duke wants to put his key in a safe place, so he puts it under his bed.

_____

b) Jamie needs to get the key from the Duke.

_____

c) The Duke doesn't wake up.

_____

d) There aren't very many prisoners in the dungeon.

_____

e) When the guards hear the Duke on Natalie's digital voice recorder, they know that he is not their friend.

_____

f) The kids and the prisoners put the Duke and the guards in the stocks.

_____

Scene 7

1. *Why can no one find the dungeon today?*

2. *What does Ricky think about a) the game on his mobile phone and b) the past?*

After reading

1. *It's the next day and the kids tell the class about their adventure. Write their dialogue.*

2. *Who said these words?*

   a) I'm so cruel. I really don't know how I do it!

   _____

   b) Mickey who?

   _____

   c) I never want to see another maze again!

   _____

   d) We know there is a dungeon, but nobody knows where it is.

   _____

   e) Get me some wood, boy!

   _____

   f) Listen, you can hear your "friend" the Duke.

   _____

   g) Let's put these two in the stocks!

   _____

3. *What do you think of the play now?*

   My favourite character in "Fenimore Castle" is

   _____ because _____

   _____.

   The best part of the play is when _____

   _____

   _____.

4. *Which time in history would you like to visit? Why? What would you do there?*

5. *Project: You want to put on the play for a parents' day at school. Make a poster and a programme. Who wants to act? Who wants to make costumes? What props do you need? Have fun!*

---

play [pleɪ] Theaterstück • **to put on** [pʊt ˈɒn] *hier:* aufführen • **programme** [ˈprəʊɡræm] Programmheft • **costume** [ˈkɒstjuːm] Kostüme • **props** [prɒps] Requisiten

How to put on plays

You must remember many things when you put a play on stage.

Here is a list to help you:

1. *Together with your teacher: choose a director and his/her team (two or three pupils). A director tells the actors how to act, what to do on stage, how to move, how to speak, etc. Don't forget that body language is very important. You can find a lot of extra information in the texts of the plays.*

2. *Choose two prompters. Prompters help the actors when they have problems with their text.*

3. *Choose the pupils who are responsible for the costumes, the sound effects, the lights and the make-up.*

4. *Make a list of things you need. You do not have much time between the scenes, so everyone must be ready and everything must be prepared.*

5. *Ask other teachers (Music, …) to help you with the preparation.*

6. *Choose two pupils to organize these things: where to put on the play (in a classroom, the school hall …); when to put it on (a school party, your school's Open Day …); who to invite (pupils, parents …); who will make flyers, programmes or posters for the play.*

---

director [dɪˈrektə] Regisseur(in) • **to move** [muːv] sich bewegen • **body language** [ˈbɒdi ˌlæŋɡwɪdʒ] Körpersprache • **prompter** [ˈprɒmtə] Soffleur (Soffleuse) • **to be responsible for** [rɪˈspɒnsəbl fə] für etw verantwortlich sein • **lights** [laits] Beleuchtung • **between** [bɪˈtwiːn] zwischen • **scene** [siːn] Szene • **to be prepared** [prɪˈpeəd] auf etw vorbereitet sein • **to organize** [ˈɔːɡnaɪz] organisieren • **school hall** [ˈskuːl hɔːl] Aula • **Open Day** [ˈəʊpn deɪ] Tag der offenen Tür

7. *Time: checking the time is very important when you want to perform. Make sure that you know how long it takes (minutes) to perform the scenes.*

8. *Music: decide if you want to have short pieces of music at the start of the play and/or between the scenes. People like music, and this gives you time to prepare/check everything for the next scene.*

For the actors:

1. *Learn your text well. If you are not prepared, the other actors will have problems, too.*

2. *Speak loudly and clearly. – The audience will hear the words only once.*

3. *Choose good costumes. They can help you to "feel" your role.*

These pages will help you to prepare the play for the stage. But there are only a few ideas here. Feel free to do what you think is best!

> *Adaptation of tips by Antje Körber from*
> *"The stage is yours" (Hrsg. Antje Körber)*
> *(ISBN: 978-3-12-547085-9)*

---

to check [tʃek] kontrollieren • **to perform** [pəˈfɔːm] aufführen • **to decide** [dɪˈsaɪd] entscheiden • **piece** [piːs] Stück • **audience** [ˈɔːdiəns] Publikum • **will** [wɪl] wird • **once** [wʌns] einmal • **feel your role** [ˌfiːl jə ˈrəʊl] dich in eine Rolle einfühlen • **feel free to do what you think is best** [fiːl ˈfriː] Mach, was du für richtig hältst

Solutions

Before you read

1. *Examples:* We can drive cars. / We can't usually live in castles. / We've got the Internet. / We don't have their funny clothes!)
2. –
3. a) *Examples:* They look nervous / scared …
   b) The Duke of Fenimore
   c) –
   d) 1. 3   2. 2

Activities

Scene 1

1. Modern things: mobile phones / TV / cars / Internet / music downloads / mobile games
2. The mystery is that no one can find the dungeon.

Scene 2

1. No, he thinks it's old and boring because there is no tour of the dungeon.
2. –
3. coach – Reisebus; entrance hall – Eingangshalle; maze – Irrgarten; dead end – Sackgasse; to leave – abfahren; something – etwas

Scene 3

1. The paintings are of the Duke of Fenimore and Padlock, his Chief of Police.
2. The key has a strange design on it.
3. Jamie takes a picture of the key so that the kids can use it like a map to find the dungeon.
4. They move the painting because the map says to go straight on. They guess that there is a door behind the painting.

Scene 4

1. The kids know that they are in the past because the castle shop and the drinks machine are gone, there are only torches and no

39

electricity, and the people they see have got on clothes from the old days.
2. Ben is the kitchen boy. He tells the kids that there is a dungeon, it's full of prisoners, and only the Duke and Padlock know where it is. Only the Duke has the key.
3. Ben doesn't know what white bread is, what tomatoes are, and he doesn't know what a watch is.

Scene 5
a) 3.   b) 2.   c) 3.   d) 2.

Scene 6
a) The Duke puts the key under his pillow.
b) Ricky gets the key.
c) Correct
d) There are many prisoners in the dungeon.
e) Correct
f) The kids, the prisoners and the guards put the Duke and Padlock in the stocks.

Scene 7
1. No one can find the tunnel today because there is a wall over it. Ben, the guards and the prisoners closed it so that no one would put people in there again.
2. a) Ricky gives Ben his mobile phone with the maze game because he never wants to see another game like that again.
   b) He doesn't think the past is so boring now.

After reading
1. –
2. a) the Duke   b) Ben   c) Ricky   d) Mr Watkins
   e) Cook   f) Natalie   g) guards
3. –
4. –
5. –

40